D1360952

Johnny Breadless
A Pacifist Fairy Tale

by Paul Vaillant-Couturier

Illustrated by de Jean Lurçat

Translated and Adapted by Jack Zipes

First published by Clarté, Paris, 1921

Designed by Martin Skoro and Ross Rezac, MartinRoss Design

Illustrated by Jean Lurçat, English version and
Paul Picart le Doux, French version

Printed by Anderberg Innovative Print Solutions

Distributed by Wayne State University Press

ISBN 978-1-7332232-0-1

Contents

Preface

The only positive effect of war is that it can transform soldiers into pacifists. This is what happened to Paul Vaillant-Couturier (1892-1937). He enlisted to fight valiantly for his beloved France in 1914 during World War I and soon realized that thousands of young men were being exploited by governments on all sides. Vaillant-Couturier hoped that people could resolve their differences without using weapons. Wounded several times, he survived the war in 1918 as a communist who sought a better, more peaceful world. Among his many activities as a journalist and politician after the so-called Great War, Vaillant-Couturier wrote a tiny book in 1921 for children so they might know more about social injustice and the people and forces that produced wars. The first edition was illustrated by Paul Picart le Doux, and it is reproduced here in French as an appendix for those readers who would like to read the original text. A second edition appeared in 1934 and was illustrated by Jean Lurçat whose images are reproduced in my English translation. Readers may find some of Vaillant-Couturier's writing somewhat didactic, but we must remember that he was one of the very first European writers ever to write specifically and honestly for children about the evils of war. His story is still relevant for our times.

Jack Zipes

There was once
a little boy called
Johnny Breadless.

Now, you might ask yourself how he happened to get this name and whether it was because he often carried tiny bread crumbs in his hands for eating. Actually, Johnny Breadless was given this name because bread was about his only food, and because he had nothing to put on it. He was as poor as a mouse. In fact, the boy was called Johnny Breadless because dry bread was the only thing he could eat. In fact, Johnny Breadless had a life so sad that he never smiled or laughed. That's just the way it was.

Johnny was blond-haired. He had a small perked nose, blue eyes, a black vest, and yellow pants. He didn't work because there was no work for him, and he didn't go to school because he was the only one to take care of his mother. This poor woman, who had struggled and toiled her entire life, suffered from a lung disease and lived in a small room down in the basement of a house where the heat went off every third day.

Johnny's father had never returned from the war after he had said good-bye to his small family. He had left his son a small aluminum ring with a copper clover that had "Verdun" engraved on the inside. All this happened in a village in the North of France in 1917 during the Great War. Johnny was ten years old at the time.

One winter evening, as he returned home with his meager supply of bread crumbs, he saw numerous people gathered in his mother's room. The priest and the owner of the house counted all the money they could find hidden in the stove and under the bed to pay for the rent and a special mass. Johnny was ashamed, and without understanding exactly what was happening, he departed. No one stopped him. It was Christmas Eve, the night when many children received beautiful gifts beneath a tree decorated with candles, strings of coins, barley sugar, candy, and dolls.

Outside, at the front door, Johnny Breadless sat down and sobbed. He wept for a long time, and after he had cried enough, he stood up because he was very cold, and he began to walk straight toward the village without knowing why.

The village was really nothing more of a village. The war had destroyed a good part of it. The roofs bit the sky with their broken teeth, and the remains of the chimneys seemed to be caving into the homes. Johnny Breadless had often walked along this road. He was familiar with all the cellars that had been broken open where he could usually find empty bottles, partially burned wood, smashed cans, torn photos, helmets, and all sorts of extraordinary things. But on this particular night Johnny Breadless did not stop anywhere.

The walls mocked him and seemed to collapse on his path. The cellars appeared to move their trap doors right to his feet. Despite all this, Johnny was not afraid of the night and did not need to whistle to give himself courage. He walked straight ahead without hesitating right to the end of the village where he approached a crossroad. When he arrived there, he saw that he had disturbed a poacher lying in wait for some prey. The man immediately fled, while Johnny stopped. He sat down on a boundary stone marking the miles, and he noticed that it had the number three. In front of him, an old field of beets spread out, and at the bottom, the woods sprouted beneath the rising moon. The forest had been demolished by the war.

Whenever he was very troubled, Johnny always went there because the plants and animals always befriended him. In the summer, he sank into the green grass or into the warm wheat and played with the grasshoppers. In the spring, he joined the large group of cricket musicians. In the winter, he searched for the great flocks of herons, larks, and ducks amid the clouds as they flew away on their voyages.

This night, it was so cold, so very cold, and when he looked around in the air, the only thing he could see were the stars in the sky that opened and closed their eyes. As he sighed deeply with regret that he couldn't go and play with them, something rustled in the frozen grass, and it soared from the field of beets in one lithe jump and landed right before him on the path,

It was a rabbit.

Johnny Breadless looked at the rabbit and didn't move.

The rabbit had stopped. Its ears stood up as if it were ready to flee, but then it seemed reassured there was no danger and didn't move. Now the rabbit sat down, gathered its tiny paws beneath its stomach to keep them warm, and flapped its ears a bit so they crisscrossed. All at once, it leapt and landed by Johnny's side.

"Good evening, Johnny," it said.

In general, if rabbits don't speak, it's because perhaps that they are never given time to talk. Often, they are scared away or hunted. So, rabbits do not trust people very much, not even little children. All this explains why they have gained a terrible reputation as cowards. And yet, rabbits are the most kind and gentle of animals, much more gentle than cats.

Johnny took off his cap and said: "Good evening, Rabbit."

Rabbit tweaked his nose and moustache with a satisfied air and turned his head toward the side of the moon.

"By chasing the poacher from here just a while ago," Rabbit declared, "you rendered all the animals of the meadows and woods a great service. . . . We have a clear night. Would you like to take a walk with me?"

"If you would like, Rabbit, but I can't promise you that I can run as fast as you can. . . ."

Rabbit began to laugh.

"Who told you that I wanted to make you run and to make myself so exhausted that I'd be caught on the path by the first nasty dog from the village before morning. Listen, Johnny. The wild animals decided this night to choose a son of the people who has never killed and to reveal some marvelous things to him. You see, the people who work need to learn to be strong and free. Your father would not have died in the war, and your mother would not have become sick if the people had been free enough and also strong. This is the reason why you've never been able to smile. When people are strong and free, they won't harm each other anymore, and perhaps they won't do anything harmful to wild animals . . . So, tonight you must get to know the truth and learn about those among us that suffer the most. Then, you, Johnny Breadless, for the first time in your short life, you will smile. . . . Now, let me look for my airplane."

Rabbit hopped away and disappeared into the field of beets.

"Your airplane?"

By this time, Johnny was already totally astonished by Rabbit's talk and had not recovered from it. Was he really going to fly in an airplane? Now, you must confess that you, too, would have been stunned because never, never-ever, in those stories in which animals speak have they been depicted in an airplane.

Johnny was delighted by the idea of flying to where the herons, larks, and ducks came from, and he was eager to fly up to the stars.

"Kerrr-ick! Kerr-ick! . . . . Vrrrrou!"

All at once, twenty partridges flew out of nowhere and landed near Johnny, twenty large gray and blue partridges with beautiful red horseshoes on their breasts. They were led by the mother partridge of partridges. The momentum of the flight made them run a moment on a frozen road until they could stop. Then they grouped themselves together with dignity on a slope.

"Kerr-ick! Kerr-ick! Good evening, Johnny!"

"Good evening, partridges," Johnny responded, as he searched in his pockets for some bread crumbs to offer them because he thought that they might be very hungry in such freezing weather. Then, all of a sudden, Rabbit hopped from the field of beets and approached Johnny.

"Just one minute more, and we'll depart on my special plane!"

Johnny searched for the airplane. He had already looked for it in the sky, on the ground, right and left, behind him, and he saw nothing. . . . You would have been as astonished as he was if you had been in his place. But his astonishment did not end there. In fact, it continued when he saw Rabbit unscrew his ears with his front paws one after the other and glued their stems together to form a superb propeller that he stuck on the beak of the mother partridge. Then he turned the propeller so that the plane began to chug. After that he used a dry leaf, turned it into a pilot's cap, and took Johnny's hand.

As he led him to the slope, he said: "All aboard! The plank of the plane is solid, and you don't weigh much. I hope you're not afraid."

"No, but where are we going?"

"You will see."

So, Johnny sat down inside the plane among the partridges who eagerly made room for him. Each one of them held the end of a long roll in its beak, and Johnny sat down in the middle of all the rolls that were linked together. Rabbit took his seat in front of Johnny and blew a whistle. Immediately, the partridges began running. They gathered speed with their paws and spread their wings so that Johnny felt himself become lighter and lighter. The wind blew more strongly. Johnny was heading toward the path of the herons, larks, and ducks.

During the take-off, Johnny had stuck his head out into the sky, and then, when they had reached a certain height, he withdrew it. He looked for the partridges and discovered the panels of the monoplane. He no longer saw the twigs but rather a fuselage and realized that he was no longer seated on fragile sticks but was in a closed cabin. Rabbit was no longer in front of him. Instead, there was a pilot dressed in a tawny fur-lined coat and wearing a pilot's leather cap. He was listening carefully to the controls and roar of the motor and setting the directions of the compass.

Johnny thought quickly that all this had to be about one of those stories that his mother used to tell him where the pumpkins become carriages, and the lizards, servants in uniforms.

It was very beautiful in the sky. Those who knew how to count would have been able to count the stars. But that would have taken too long. The moon was much larger than Johnny thought. It was an enormous eye with spots. During the night he discovered some very astonishing things—a long white streak like a wedding dress with all kinds of glittering spangles and red stars, some others, green and blue. Certain stars appeared to be held by invisible hands to form circles, figures, and designs. From time to time, one or more of the stars detached themselves from the others, zooming off to dance somewhere else. Some of them, all by themselves, very proud, glistened separately, as though they were vexed by the vulgar brightness that the great lantern of the moon expended.

But, suddenly, the moon seemed to fade. A faint light rose from the earth and soaked the airplane causing it to descend at full speed toward the lights. Johnny closed his eyes because the plane was clearly going too fast. When he reopened his eyes, he found his rear end was sitting on a flat roof surrounded by twenty partridges pecking all around them, and Rabbit, hopping about.

Johnny stood up, looked, and listened.

If you could have only heard the noise!

Johnny was overcome by the whistling of the locomotives, the fumes of smoke, the roaring of machines, and the explosions of motors. In the red night the rumbling of the furnaces were flaming where cast iron was melting. Immense brick and iron towers seemed to be burning. On the ground the rails gleamed, crossed over themselves, and twisted themselves around like grass snakes beneath the thousands of electric lamps. The trucks followed one after the other; the cars of the trains, one after the other; the locomotives one after the other. The long black trains travelled into the countryside puffing and panting, and the trucks rolled on the roads like iron elephants.

There was a roof of clear glass beneath Johnny's feet below, and the roof vibrated so much that it tickled the bottom of his feet. The partridges flew about as though they were afraid of burning their feet, and Rabbit's belly was illuminated so that it appeared to be wearing a white vest. Johnny would have liked to have known what he was wearing below the vest, but the glass roof was painted gray, and he could see nothing through it.

A few steps away there was a trapdoor, a certain kind of window that people called a skylight, and it was open, and a large ray of light emanated from where the dust was dancing. Johnny approached the skylight and wanted to see what was there. But he had hardly glanced below the window when he felt sick, totally sick.

A breath of hot and drab air blew onto his nose. It smelled bad. It smelled like sweat, grime, burned oil, a wet dog, cooked leather, and all the most disgusting odors that you might imagine, but concentrated.

"Make an effort, little Johnny. . . . It is in the air just like this that millions of people must live like you," Rabbit said.

"And what bad things have they done to deserve something like this?"

"Nothing. They are just poor. It was under conditions like this that your mother and many other mothers became sick."

Johnny pinched his nose with one hand, covered his mouth with the other, and looked. At first, he could only see a blue mist. Then he was able to distinguish the moving belts. Finally, he was able to perceive the machines, hundreds of machines and mechanical parts that thumped, drilled, cut, turned, rolled, flattened, thinned, went, came, slid, and creaked beneath the lights.

"That's the factory," Johnny said.

And since he knew that the machines did not work by themselves, he began to look for the people who made them work. It was not easy to see them. They were dripping with so much sweat and so gray that Johnny at first confused them with the machines. It seemed that the machines made them work, just like marionettes which always make the same movements when their strings are pulled. Johnny tried to count them with his fingers, but he only knew how to count up to five, and the only thing he could say was that there were much more than five.

Since the work the people were doing interested him, he looked for a particular person he could study while she was working. After he chose one, he didn't know whether he had selected a woman or a man. This person was pale and wearing a large blue shirt and headband. He coughed severely, and from time to time, he hid and wiped his mouth with his handkerchief. He worked beneath an enormous ventilator, and the wind of the ventilator sometimes lifted a part of the man's cap.

Johnny chose to focus on this person because he resembled his father a little and because he coughed like his mother.

"That worker you're looking at," Rabbit began to say—

"Ah! I know. It's a woman," Johnny said.

"Yes, she's the daughter of a miner," Rabbit told her. "Her name is Marie. Her father died at the bottom of a mine when everything exploded. She worked in a weaving mill for a long time, and then, when the war started and her factory was demolished, she took a job in a gas workshop to earn money and nourish her children. However, she herself became sick. The gas poisoned the workers who manufactured it. She had wanted to protect the other workers, protect them against the poison produced by the syndicate. She was fired from this job by her boss who told other heads of corporations not to hire her if she came looking for a job. She was only able to find work here because an old foreman had thought that she would not cause any problems because of her miserable situation. Still, they threatened her every day. . . . And you see, Johnny, she must also take care of three little daughters while her husband is still fighting in the war. All the other people who are working with her are as poor as she is and work long hours as she does into the night until they fall. . . . And when they become old, they are thrown out of the factory without bread and a roof over their heads."

Johnny wanted to descend into the middle of the mill and embrace Marie who was so good, poor, and sick. He also wanted to embrace the other workers and tell them about his mother. Then, suddenly he heard a cry that pierced the regular noise of the machines, and he saw Marie snatched from the floor and carried by the large ventilator and then dropped to the ground like a broken wreck. She didn't move.

Johnny took a few steps back and shouted, "Let's get away from here. Let's leave, Rabbit! You fooled me when you said that you would make me smile and laugh. All the mothers and fathers are treated much too badly here. . . . Let's leave!"

"Even so," said Rabbit, "keep in mind, this is the life waiting for the poor children."

Then Johnny Breadless moved his head toward Rabbit's warm and soft chest and began to sob. But there was also a great deal of anger in his sorrow.

What happened to him? How did the airplane depart again? How and where did he land? Johnny was too troubled to think about all this, and you can imagine how he felt, if you will.

What is certain is that Johnny Breadless covered his eyes once again with his hands and soon found himself in the middle of a splendid mansion. It was beautiful! It was truly beautiful! Actually, no. It was more than beautiful! It was golden!

On the ceiling blue and rose-colored ladies flew among little cupids carrying bouquets of flowers. Down below there were flowers everywhere and small tables covered with very stiff and white cloths overloaded with gold, silver, crystals and dishes so transparent that one could see everything right through them. The glasses had the color of soap bubbles.

Very few boys and girls had ever seen such things, and even these children were rare. This was because there are very few people rich enough to view these things and also because even the very rich people are ashamed to bring others to the places inhabited by their children. They go there only to hide their terrible greed.

Behind each table there was a gentleman in a black and white tuxedo who served things to eat and continually bowed. There were pâtés, beautiful crunchy pâtés and glittering dishes of partridges, pheasants, and stuffed peacocks. There were roasted chickens, gilded from head to toe, and there were all sorts of roasted meat as well as all kinds of fish from whale to red fish. There were different kinds of ice cream—strawberry, peach, pistachio, apricot, and vanilla as well as rose and mixed ice cream. There was chocolate cream, and there were cakes all with different names and from many different countries – éclair, mixed pastry, puff pastry, sponge finger cakes, tarts, soufflés, shortcut pastry, apple turnovers, pound cake, almond paste, gingerbread, barnacle goose, cookies, puits d'amour, batons de Jacob, doughnuts, and rum babas. There were small houses made of nougat and pyramids made of jam. There was fruit from every season. There was even a black ragout called stew that made a very bad impression on Rabbit. But what attracted Johnny most of all was the bread.

There were long loaves of white bread, you know, but whiter than the whitest cakes. The bread smelled good and was crisp and well done. Johnny's nose grew longer. And it began to shine. It glistened everywhere.

At first, the lamps glittered, and then the chandeliers and glass on the walls began to glitter. Next came the carafes that glistened, and the ladies appeared to want to glisten more than the carafes. They were covered with diamonds trimmed like the corks of the carafes.

The gentlemen also glistened. Some because of the monocles they were wearing, others because of their bald skulls or their shirts. All of them had rings made of diverse colors. There were officers from many different countries wearing stripes, crosses, and medals spread on their chests like kitchen utensils attached to their red, green, blue, or yellow garters. It seemed that they had the desire to enchant the entire world and show off their wealth. And each and everyone who gathered before the tables resembled the most nasty or the most stupid of the stupid people wearing their jewels and beautiful clothes.

There was a gentleman with rosy cheeks, a bald head, and greasy skin, and another gentleman with thick lips, a large round nose, and tiny eyes lost in his greasy skin, who bumped into the first man and gave him three slaps on the back. This gentleman resembled an exhausted pig.

There was another thin man with a long yellow face beneath a crew cut. He had a long nose with a monocle, slick lips, eyes uplifted, and pointed ears. You would have sworn that he was a jackass.

Another sort of man was wearing a violet robe and carried a golden cross on his watch chain. He had large round eyes that popped out on his face, an enormous grin from ear to ear, and a chin, which extended to his waist. He kept opening his mouth all the time like a toad suffering from the heat.

There was also a general in a grand black uniform with red pants. He was so enormous that he could crack any chair in which he sat. This general had a brick-red face beneath uneven, enormous white eyebrows, and his moustache was thick and yellow. He looked as if he slept all the time, but perhaps he didn't sleep. He was busy digesting all that he had eaten. You would have thought that he had eaten greasy meat.

There were also loads of ladies and gentlemen who resembled geese, giraffes, and lizards. The men looked like apes, turkeys, goats, tigers, crocodiles, and wolves. And they all ate, drank, and laughed. It was a scene not to be missed.

Johnny, Rabbit, and the partridges took refuge beneath a table where nobody was eating, and they looked at the scene from this spot below the table cloth.

"They must work an awful lot in their factories to be able to have money and eat like this!" Johnny said with admiration.

"That's where they're cheating you, Johnny!"

"How?"

"It's because they don't work and earn money to eat like that."

"Ah! Well then, how do they do that? How do they cheat?"

"Yes, they cheat. That's to say, they steal."

"That's really bad."

"That's how it is," Rabbit said. "Just take a look at the gentleman who resembles a large exhausted pig. Do you see him with the red flower stuck in his button hole and smoking his large cigar?"

"Yes."

"Well he's Marie's boss, you know, Marie, from the factory."

"Oh, well, we've got to be quick and tell him what happened. Then he'll take his plane or car and go to the workshop to take care of her."

"If only you knew how you're just wasting his time! He doesn't even know her, and if he knew her, he would fire her."

"Oh!" Johnny said indignantly. "He's a mean person."

"No," Rabbit replied. "He's a boss."

"Ah! Is that the same thing?"

"It's even worse!" And the rabbit continued. "Do you see the general who resembles a large ox and looks like he's sleeping beneath his medals. He's the one who's in charge of the war."

"But, the war's not here. It's on the front."

"For him, the war is here. He himself never fights. But he has others fight for him. He just eats and sleeps. Between you and me, the generals never fight."

"So, he's a swindler as well?"

"That's how he causes so many fathers to die."

"Ah? Then he's also mean?"

"No," Rabbit responded. "He's a general, and that man over there with the violet robe and large belly who resembles a toad. That's a bishop. In order to trick poor people, his religion tells him that he must be poor and love all people, but that man there orders soldiers to kill their brothers, and he is very rich."

"Swindler! Lousy swindler!" Johnny exclaimed, and once again, he became angry.

"And that one over there," Rabbit pointed, "the one who looks like a jackass, do you see him?'

"Yes."

"He's a minister."

Johnny would have asked the Rabbit for other explanations if something extraordinary had not happened at this precise moment.

"Crack! Boom!"

The general had eaten and drunk so much that he fell asleep, and his chair had decided no longer to carry his weight. It was totally destroyed.

"Crack! Bam!"

The general fell to the ground, sound asleep, dragging the table cloth, the forks, the napkins, bottles and a plate of cream with him. All this was spread on his enormous stomach.

As people rushed from all sides to help the bombastic officer, who was unable to stand on his feet himself, Johnny pulled the table cloth from him and addressed one of the servants dressed in a black tuxedo,

"Did he hurt himself, the swindler?" he asked.

In response, and before he could even make one move, Johnny Breadless received an enormous slap that sent him rolling for about ten feet. He hardly had time to get up on his feet when he saw a bunch of men in black tuxedos, officers with sabers, and ladies with sharp nails in front of him. And they all cried out: "Arrest him! It's him, the beggar! He's the one who knocked down our general! Arrest him! Run and search for the city guards!"

Upon hearing these words, Johnny Breadless thought he was lost. He fortunately grabbed hold of Rabbit by the fur on his neck.

"Hold on tight," said Rabbit, and all at once he began to gallop, sweeping up Johnny as he set off on his mad dash. In the meantime, the partridges made a terrible noise and flew away, breaking the dishes, smashing the glasses, and exploding the electric lamps that they encountered.

"Vrrrrrr! Bam! Bam!"

The officers believed that a bombardment had begun, and they immediately took refuge under the tables. The ladies fainted. The partridges followed Johnny and Rabbit, and from time to time, they hit anyone who tried to stop them. They slapped them in the face with hard whacks of their wings and sharp pecks with their beaks.

"Kerrr-ick! I'm going to peck you! Kerrr-ick! I'm going to strike you!"

And Johnny ran, and he ran, and he ran. Sometimes he was on his feet, other times he was on his tummy, or on his rear end, and finally he was riding horseback on the back of Rabbit.

Then Johnny jumped into a hallway and climbed some stairs. Next he went down some other stairs. He crossed through the kitchens where the cooks became so frightened that they spilled the sauces and plunged into the pots. Finally, Johnny found the door, pursued by the same angry people who had dashed after him into the street. But no sooner was he outside than all the partridges gathered around Johnny and, in front of the furious and astonished ladies, men in tuxedos, officers and sergeants of the city, they lifted him and Rabbit straight up into the moonlight.

Caroom! Boom! Boom! Boom! Tatatatatatatac! Ziiiiiiiiiit! Clack! Zoom! Zooom!"

The earth was exploding.

Now they were right at the front lines of the war. It was dreadful and freezing. Johnny Breadless's teeth were chattering, and he was shivering in the middle of terrifying noise. The wind slapped his cheeks, and they were burning, but he barely thought about this because he saw terrible and ugly things. Johnny, Rabbit, and the partridges walked very fast, jumping from one trench to another, from frozen mud to ice, and from ice to the frozen mud. Johnny kept falling. The soldiers fell on the battlefield all the time because there were all sorts of things that caught hold of their feet.

"Who's that dirty little kid? What's he doing here?" one of the soldiers yelled with his beard spread beneath the barbed wire.

And bam! He got tangled up in Johnny's feet.

"Where did this kid come from?" asked the ice that had formed one the edges of the trenches. "I'll gladly crunch him especially because he's so tender."

And, suddenly, "Crack!" The ice opened beneath Johnny's feet.

"Well, well, here's a little bug that I'd gladly change into pulp for the crows," said a large bomb shell that was fully congested and furious because it hadn't exploded. "If only he would touch me on the right spot!"

And, "Bing!" The shell set out after Johnny.

"Ah, hah!" the bayonet said. "This is good! Just look at the pretty little feet with torn shoes. I'll make the feet bleed!"

And, "Pick-pick!" The bayonet punched its way through the soles of Johnny's shoes. To avoid stepping on the bomb shells, falling on the barbed wire, having his feet pierced by bayonets, and to sink into the ice, Johnny felt a fierce desire to run from the battlefield. However, he didn't dare admit this,

"Ho! Ho! You dirty kid," the mustard gas said, still hanging in tatters on the grass. "Stay there while I make a brief visit in your lungs."

And, "Hissssss!" The greenish poison gas tried to hiss through Johnny's lips. His nose was bloody, his hands were raw, his feet, soaking wet, his eyes full of tears, his vest in tatters, his yellow pants ripped apart. But Rabbit and the partridges kept marching onward, and Johnny did not want to lose them.

"Is the war going to last much longer?" Johnny asked.

"Yes, it's going to last for miles and miles and years and years," Rabbit responded, "It will last until the soldiers want it to stop."

And Johnny and his friends kept on walking. Sometimes missiles soared in the sky, and everything became white as if someone had spilled flour on the moon. At a moment like this the soldiers had to throw themselves down on the ground no matter where – on the ice or on the barbed wire. And the bullets whistled on all sides seeking to bite some one.

"Phooey! Where is he?"

"Zummmm! I'm searching for him!

"Tac! Missed!"

"Zilou! Flof! I scored a hit on ground."

"Tacatacatactacataca!"

"Nobody is going to pass here!"

The missiles stopped coming, and they were able to set out again. They crossed bridges, and along the way there were black and stinking ditches where nothing appeared to be able to live.

"The trenches," Rabbit said.

Then they again encountered the barbed wire, the holes, and the bumps. Johnny stopped at one place. There were many men there, some were lying down, others were on their knees. One of them seemed to be setting up barbed wire.

"Is he an enemy?" Johnny whispered to Rabbit.

"No."

"Ah!"

Johnny approached the soldier who was caught in the barbed wire. When he was very close, he stopped and waited. The man didn't move. Johnny didn't dare call to him. A missile soared. Johnny opened his eyes as best he could. The man's lips formed a grimace, and there was a small black hole in the middle of his forehead topping a green face.

Johnny cried out, jumped backwards, and tumbled down through barbed wire into a trench, where the partridges and Rabbit had gathered together. He was completely pale and had red cuts, totally frozen beneath his tattered clothes.

"Who's that?" he asked. "Who's the man over there?"

"It's a father who was hit in the head by one of those tiny bullets that you heard whistle by you. If he could have survived and gone on to teach, he would have become a great scholar later on."

"Well then, why is he there?"

"Because he was poor, and the fat general who ate so much ordered him to be there."

"The swindler?"

"Yes. And also this man had to be there so he could make the fat gentleman richer. I mean the man who resembled an exhausted hog."

"The boss."

"Yes. This was also the reason why the big yellow man voted for the war, the one who resembled a jackass."

"The minister?"

"Yes. And all this was done with the blessing of the toad in the violet robe."

"The bishop."

"That's right."

Johnny began to shiver a great deal. Then the partridges huddled around him. They clambered to his neck, his chest, his stomach, and his legs and opened their small wings to make a good feather cover while Rabbit slid behind his head like a cuddly pillow warm and soft.

The bullets continued to whistle by him, and the shells barked.

"Bow Wow!"

Johnny Breadless opened his eyes. Everything had become white.

"Let's get out of here!" he cried. "This isn't the place where I can smile and laugh. Let's go, Rabbit!"

"Wait a second. Are you feeling better?" Rabbit asked. "Are you warmer now?"

"Yes."

"Then, listen. While you were sleeping, we did some exploring. On our way we passed flowing and frozen rivers down below, mountains, great plains, and cities. We've covered hundreds and hundreds of miles and have flown toward the north. Now we are in the snowy countries."

"But is the war still going on here?"

"Yes, but not for a long time. Soon the missiles will stop exploding and the bullets will stop whistling. The shells will stop exploding. At midnight there will be a cease fire on both sides."

"Why?"

"Because the soldiers have had enough and want to talk."

As they waited, the duel of the canons intensified and became twice as violent. While standing there, Johnny held his breath until midnight. Then, all of a sudden, there was total silence, a silence so great that one could almost hear the snow flakes fall. In the distance, a clock sounded. It was far, far away.

The twenty partridges, who were behind Rabbit, cautiously stuck their beaks outside.

"You can come, Johnny," Rabbit said.

Johnny climbed out of the trench. There he was, standing on top of a heap of snow and a full moon shining down on him. Johnny looked to the left and the right. The only thing he saw was the frozen snow with gray lines that disappeared into the night. He seemed well, and as he looked and could see more clearly, he noticed something move to his right, and then to his left. On the right, something was definitely stirring. The moon revealed a pale face beneath a helmet, and half the body of a man climbed out of the trench. Then other heads appeared, and other helmets, and round caps. To the left, timid black forms appeared on the snow. There were also helmets, flat helmets. Suddenly, it seemed to Johnny that a song arose from the two sides.

"Comrades! Comrades! Comrades!"

Then there was silence. Now the men stood on the high railings without their weapons. They looked at each other. It was the first time that they had even seen each other. Johnny asked himself what they were going to do.

The men reached out to each other with their arms. Johnny was standing between the lines. Perhaps the soldiers didn't see him yet. But, suddenly, Johnny felt happy, very happy. His little chapped lips opened. Dimples appeared in his gaunt and scarred cheeks. And so it was that Johnny's small frozen face began to smile.

Johnny Breadless smiled.

It was the first time in his life that he smiled. And this smile brought a great deal of light to his face, and his eyes shone so strongly and his hair absorbed so much of the moon's rays that a great brightness spread around him.

The amazed soldiers approached from both sides at the same time. Then they crawled under the barbed wire through the snow until they came close to Johnny and kneeled before him. Some of the soldiers embraced his little hands, his tiny aluminum ring, torn vest and his bloody feet. They didn't hurt him. Nor did they harm Rabbit and the partridges. On the contrary, they greeted them politely.

"Why are you kneeling?" Johnny asked.

But they didn't understand Johnny because they didn't speak his language.

"My name's Johnny Breadless. My papa didn't return from the war. My mama collapsed yesterday, and I'm ten years old."

The men stood up and hugged Johnny. They understood two words: "papa" and "mama." Then they showed Johnny the photos of their little sons and their daughters, their fiancées and their mothers. They showed all they carried in their threadbare pockets. It was so good to find a small boy on the battleground who smiled. Rabbit translated everything for Johnny.

"Me, my name's Henry the Poor, and I was born in Munich, Germany," a German soldier said as he took off his large helmet. "I have a little daughter who's embroidering flowers while she's waiting for me. But perhaps she may never get to see me."

"Me, my name's Ivan the Unfortunate, and I was born near Moscow in Russia," a Russian soldier said. "I've an old mama, who's weeping and waiting for me in a village. Perhaps I'll never return and see her again."

"Why not?" Johnny asked. He really wanted to return Henry to his little daughter and Ivan to his old mama.

"Because they are hurting us."

"Who are the people hurting you, Henry?"

Henry the poor pointed with his finger at the soldier called Ivan the Unfortunate.

"And who's harming you, Ivan?"

Ivan the Unfortunate pointed with this finger at Henry the Poor.

"Are you then both mean?" Johnny asked.

"Oh, no!" Ivan and Henry replied at the same time. "On the contrary,

we both love each other. We're bringing each other gifts this night as a sign of friendship."

And Johnny watched Ivan take a large piece of bread from his pocket while Henry gave Ivan a full pack of tobacco.

"Well?" Johnny said. "I don't understand anymore. What I see is that you are brothers, both of you."

All of a sudden, a sad and muffled murmur skimmed through the ranks of the soldiers.

"It's the war,"

"But why is it the war?" Johnny asked.

No one responded. The soldiers lowered their heads and didn't dare to look at one another. And just then Johnny recalled the machine that had shattered Marie, the poison air that had a bad effect on the workers, the large boss who resembled a pig, the bishop gaping like a toad, the foolish minister who resembled a jackass, the general falling like a fat ox, and the hideous horrible battleground. And since the soldiers kept silent, Johnny asked: "And what if all the poor people and the soldiers in the world got along like this evening?"

"Well, then that would change everything," the soldiers replied.

"Then it must change!" Johnny Breadless cried. "But watch out for the swindlers!" And he tightened his small fists. "All this will change!"

Finally, one man stepped out from the group of Russian soldiers and began speaking: "Lenin said . . . ."

And one of the men among the German soldiers replied: "Liebknecht. . . ."

All at once the song of the "International" burst out. All along the trenches you could hear the cries: "Down with the war!" and "Bring on the Revolution!"

They wept. They laughed. They talked about their mothers, wives, and children. They made fists toward the past night where the generals had caroused and had a feast. No longer did they call each other with names such as the "German Krauts" or the "Bumbling Ruski." They were all brothers.

Johnny's pockets were now stuffed with chocolate and soldier's bread. There was even a tiny box of strawberry jam. All at once, Johnny Breadless laughed.

The moon also laughed out of happiness.

The barbed wire withdrew with disgust and went underground.

The old rusty shells broke open in the mud

The canons turned around and pointed themselves toward the rear.

The rifles aimed at the chiefs of staff.

The three-colored flags were torn.

The sun rose in the East like an enormous red flag.

The partridges formed a circle and sang while Rabbit danced in the middle, sometimes on his front paws, sometimes on his rear paws, he danced around Johnny Breadless, who could not stop smiling.

You'll ask me now what became of Johnny, and what became of Rabbit and the partridges, and of course what became of the soldiers and the swindlers.

Well, let me tell you that Rabbit had all the airplanes in the entire world come to this spot. Then he had each one of the soldiers seated on a monoplane that could fly a thousand miles an hour. Then they took off and headed far away toward the countries of the East. Along the way the snow fell and did not stop until daybreak.

The plane landed on a terrace. It was a palace circled by funny-looking churches with steeples in the form of onions. The rooms of the palace were gilded and radiant and covered with sculpted eagles. The tables were also covered with good things such as patés, roasted beef, pork, cakes and wine in carafes. The ceilings were completely decorated with ladies dressed in blue and red, and little cupids carried bouquets of flowers to them. There were all kinds of people who resembled those Johnny had seen at the beginning of the evening in the room where the general had tumbled to the ground.

Now, in this room there were officers from all the countries of the world and beautiful ladies in black and embroidered gowns. And all these people could do nothing more than drink, eat, and dance.

"Are they the same people?" Johnny asked.

"Just about," Rabbit responded.

And this was true. There was a large gentleman who was rosy and bald with three necks superimposed, and he resembled an exhausted pig. There was another gentleman who had a long yellow face with a crew cut and pointy ears who seemed to be a jackass. There was also a toad-like bishop enormously fat with a large blonde beard and long hair, a bit greasy as if it had been soaked in the sauces.

There was a general in a grand uniform with medals attached all over him and with golden shoulder pads. He was a chubby general dressed in green with a sort of musty yellow moustache. And he was just like a fat ox.

Ah! If you could have only seen the faces of all the people there when Johnny entered the room with his friends!

At first, the quails, the partridges, the pheasants, the grouse, and the stuffed peacocks, which were on the plates, took flight and joined the partridges who were escorting Johnny. And I assure you that this caused a huge racket among the illustrious people. They stood up in a flash, dropped their serviettes, and began to move toward the end of the room. They were terrified and livid.

This time Johnny Breadless no longer smiled. He laughed. Ah! You can't imagine how much he laughed!

"Just look, my friends!" he cried out. "Those swindlers are afraid of us now!"

Right behind Johnny were the soldiers, the workers, and the sailors, all with bayonets fixed. Each one had a red rosette on his cap. To the left of Johnny, Rabbit was sitting on his rear end with his paws crossed across his chest. To the right of Johnny, there was a big and strong soldier carrying an enormous pistol in a holster on his side. He moved toward the swindlers and said: "My name is Ivan the Unfortunate, and in the name of the Committee of Soldiers of the army of the North, I am placing all the people gathered here under arrest."

Johnny clapped his hands. The swindlers, all those who had caused Marie to die in the factory, all those who had caused fathers to die on the front lines, all those who had voted for the war, and all those who had blessed the massacre of the poor people to profit the rich people, were going to go to prison.

The swindlers trembled, turned green and collapsed at each new word spoken by the soldier. It was warm, and yet they shivered. The general surrendered his saber and his dinner. The boss asked for permission to go to his office. The bishop made the sign of the cross with his two hands and became muddled. The minister with the long ears wept with tears that kept drip-dropping all the time.

As for the beautiful ladies, they cried out, threw themselves on their knees, crawled on the ground, and offered their rings, necklaces, and pearls to Johnny and his friends. Nothing doing! Only the peacocks, the pheasants, and the partridges went to look at the pearls. They pecked with their beaks to see if the pearls were grains of wheat and then turned away with disgust when they realized this was not the case.

"Let's leave," Johnny said. He hadn't stopped laughing, and this was the boy who had never smiled. "Let's leave, Rabbit. We've got to go quickly and tell this to all the soldiers of the world!"

"Yes," Rabbit replied. "But remember that the soldiers stopped the war here."

"When I grow up," Johnny Breadless said, "and the swindlers want to begin again, I'll do what the soldiers have done!"

Whoever does not work should not eat.

Jean-sans-pain

histoire pour tous les enfants

Racontée par

Paul Vaillant Couturier

devant des images de

Picart le Doux

prix : 15 fr.

1921

Édité par "*CLARTÉ*"
16, Rue Jacques-Callot, 16
. . . . PARIS (6e) . . . .

histoire pour

tous les enfants

Jean-sans-pain

Racontée par

Paul Vaillant Couturier

devant des images de

Picart le Doux

C'ETAIT un petit garçon qu'on appelait Jean-sans-Pain.

Tu l'aurais vu que tu te serais demandé pourquoi, car il tenait presque toujours un croûton entre ses doigts.

On l'appelait Jean-sans-Pain parce que le pain sec qui était à peu près sa seule nourriture, il fallait qu'il le mendiât. Il était tout à fait pauvre.

On l'appelait Jean-sans-Pain parce qu'il ne pouvait manger que du pain.

Jean-sans-Pain avait une vie si triste qu'il n'avait jamais souri, ni ri.

C'est rare un petit garçon qui n'a jamais souri, ni ri ; pourtant, c'était comme ça. Jean était blond. Il avait un petit nez en l'air, des yeux bleus, un tablier noir et un pantalon jaune. Il ne travaillait pas parce qu'il n'y avait pas de travail pour lui et il n'allait pas à l'école parce qu'il était seul pour soigner sa maman, sa pauvre femme de maman, une ouvrière souffrant au fond d'une maison, de ses deux poumons, dans une chambre basse où le feu était éteint un jour sur trois.

Son papa n'était jamais revenu de la guerre après sa permission.

Il lui avait laissé cette fois-là une petite bague en aluminium avec un trèfle en cuivre et « Verdun » gravé à l'intérieur.

Ça se passait dans un village du Nord, pendant la guerre, et Jean-sans-Pain avait dix ans.

Un soir d'hiver, comme Jean-sans-Pain rentrait à la maison avec sa provision de croûtons, il vit beaucoup de monde dans la chambre de sa maman. Le curé comptait avec le propriétaire l'argent qu'on pourrait tirer du poêle et du lit, pour payer le loyer et la messe. Jean-sans-Pain eut honte et, sans bien comprendre, il sortit. Personne ne l'en empêcha. Or, c'était le soir de Noël, le soir où les enfants reçoivent de beaux cadeaux sous des arbres pleins de bougies, de fils d'argent, de sucre d'orge, de bonbons et de poupées.

Devant la porte, assis sur la pierre, Jean pleura beaucoup, il pleura longtemps, et quand il eut bien pleuré, il se leva, parce qu'il avait très froid, et se mit à marcher tout droit devant lui, sans savoir pourquoi.

Le village n'était plus que la moitié d'un village. La guerre l'avait abîmé... Des toits mordaient le ciel avec leurs dents cassées et des restes de cheminées avaient l'air de tirer dedans.

Jean-sans-Pain suivait ce chemin-là tous les jours. Il connaissait toutes les caves crevées où l'on trouvait des bouteilles vides, des boîtes de conserves défoncées, des casques et toutes sortes de choses extraordinaires...

Mais cette nuit-là, Jean-sans-Pain ne s'arrêtait nulle part...

Les murs se moquaient de lui et faisaient semblant de s'effondrer sur son passage, les caves avançaient leurs trappes jusqu'au bord de ses pieds.

Mais Jean n'avait pas peur de la nuit et il n'avait pas besoin de siffler pour se donner du courage. Il marcha sans hésiter jusqu'à la sortie du village, là où les chemins se croisaient.

Il vit, en avançant, qu'il avait dérangé un braconnier à l'affût, qui s'en fut...

Il s'arrêta. Il s'assit sur une borne kilométrique qui portait le chiffre 3 et regarda.

Devant lui s'étendait un ancien champ de betteraves et au fond, sur la lune qui se levait, se dressait un bois que la guerre avait tout déchiré.

Quand il avait une grosse peine, c'était toujours là que Jean venait, parce qu'il y avait là des plantes et des bêtes qui lui donnaient toujours leur amitié...

En été il s'enfonçait dans l'herbe verte ou dans les blés chauds et jouait avec les sauterelles ; en hiver, il cherchait entre les nuages les grands vols de hérons, d'alouettes et de canards qui partaient pour des voyages...

Ce soir-là, si froid, si froid, il avait beau regarder en l'air il ne voyait rien que les étoiles du ciel qui ouvraient et fermaient les yeux.

Comme il soupirait profondément du regret de ne pouvoir aller jouer avec elles, quelque chose froissa les herbes gelées et, du champ de betteraves, sauta d'un bond souple devant lui, sur les pavés.

C'était un lièvre...

Jean-sans-Pain baissa les yeux, regarda le lièvre et ne bougea pas.

Le lièvre, qui s'était arrêté les oreilles dressées, prêt à s'enfuir, semble rassuré par l'immobilité de Jean.

Il s'assoit, ramène ses petites pattes de devant sous son ventre pour les tenir au chaud, s'installe en se rengorgeant à côté de Jean et lui dit :

— Bonsoir, Jean.

En général, si les lièvres ne parlent pas, c'est qu'on ne leur en laisse pas le temps... On leur fait peur ou on les chasse. Alors les lièvres se méfient beaucoup des hommes et même des petits garçons. C'est ce qui leur vaut une terrible réputation de poltrons.

Et pourtant les lièvres sont des bêtes beaucoup plus gentilles que les chats.

Jean enlève sa casquette et dit :

— Bonsoir, Lièvre.

Le lièvre retrousse sa moustache d'un air satisfait et tourne la tête du côté de la lune :

— En chassant d'ici ce braconnier, tout à l'heure, tu as rendu à tout le gibier de la plaine et du bois un fier service... Nous avons une nuit claire... Veux-tu faire une promenade avec moi ?

— Si tu veux, lièvre, mais je ne te promets pas de courir aussi vite que toi...

Le lièvre se met à rire...

— Qui t'a dit que je voulais te faire courir et me fatiguer moi-même, pour être pris à la course, demain, par le premier roquet venu du village. Ecoute, Jean. Les bêtes des champs ont décidé ce soir de choisir un fils des hommes qui n'aurait jamais tué, ni mangé de bêtes des champs, pour lui faire connaître des choses merveilleuses. Les hommes doivent apprendre à être bons et à êtres libres. Ton papa n'est resté à la guerre et ta maman n'a eu mal que parce que les hommes ne sont encore ni assez libres, ni assez bons. C'est pour cela que tu n'as jamais pu sourire.

« Quand ils seront bons et libres, ils ne se feront plus

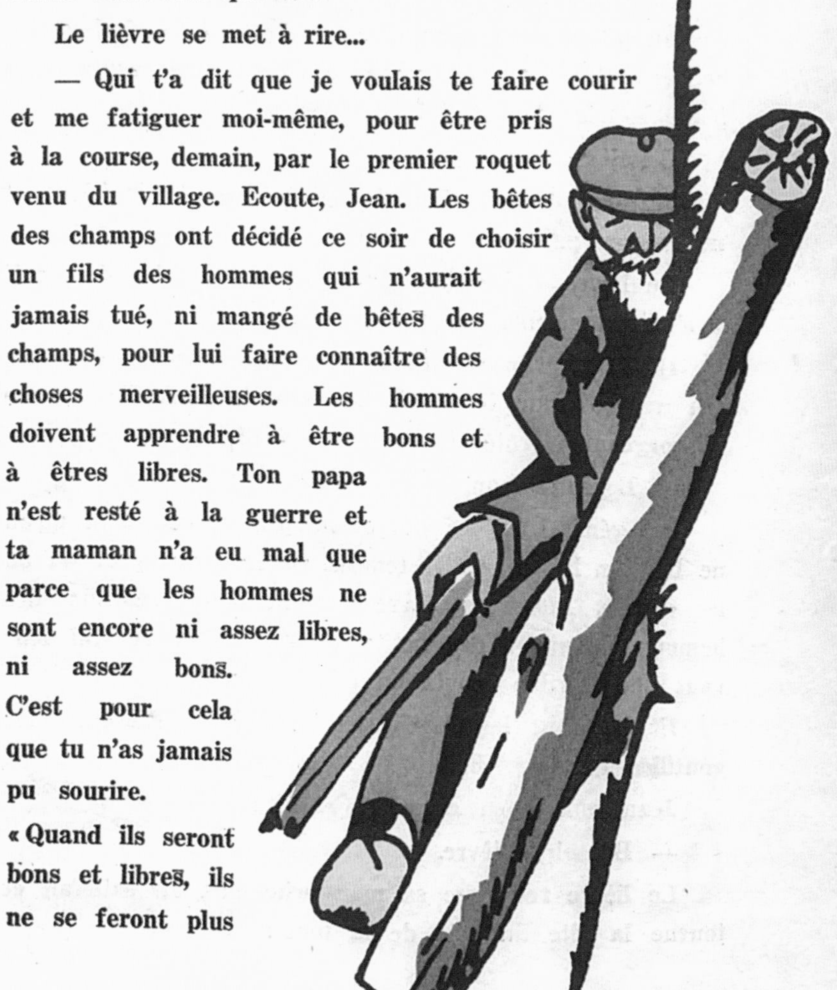

de mal entre eux et ils ne feront plus de mal aux bêtes des champs.

« C'est toi qui dois apprendre ce soir la vérité à ceux d'entre eux qui souffrent le plus. Et alors, toi, Jean-sans-Pain, pour la première fois de ta petite vie, tu souriras.

« Laisse-moi chercher mon aéroplane...

Le lièvre fait un bond et disparaît dans le champ de betteraves.

— Ton aéroplane !

A ce coup-ci, Jean, que les discours du lièvre avaient déjà rempli d'étonnement, n'en revenait plus. Il allait partir en aéroplane ! Et tu m'avoueras que tu n'en serais pas revenu non plus parce que jamais, jamais dans les histoires où parlent les bêtes, elles ne sont, jusqu'à présent, montées en aéroplane.

Ça tient tout simplement à ce que depuis très longtemps on n'a plus causé avec les bêtes. Alors on n'est plus très au courant.

Jean était ravi à l'idée d'aller où vont les hérons, les alouettes et les canards et il ne désespérait pas de monter jusqu'aux étoiles.

— Ka-tchouic ! Ka-tchouic... Vrrrrou !

Vingt perdreaux venaient maintenant de se poser devant Jean, vingt gros perdreaux gris et bleus, avec un beau fer à cheval rouge sur la poitrine...

L'élan du vol les fit courir un moment sur la route d'un air affairé. Puis ils se groupèrent bien dignement sur le talus.

— Katchouic ! Katchouic ! Bonjour, Jean !

— Bonjour, perdreaux, répondit Jean.

Et il chercha dans ses poches des mies de pain pour les leur offrir, car il pensa qu'avec un froid pareil ils devaient avoir bien faim.

Soudain le lièvre bondit hors des betteraves et s'approcha de Jean.

— Une minute encore et l'on part sur mon appareil !

Jean cherchait l'aéroplane. Il avait beau regarder en l'air, par terre, à droite, à gauche, derrière lui, il ne voyait rien... Tu aurais été étonné comme lui, à sa place. Mais, où sa stupeur fut complète, ce fut quand il vit le lièvre dévisser l'une après l'autre ses oreilles avec ses pattes et les collant bout à bout en faire une superbe hélice qu'il fixa au bec de l'un des perdreaux et qu'il fit tourner en soufflant dessus.

Après quoi, s'étant adapté une feuille sèche sur la tête pour s'en faire un bonnet d'aviateur, il prit Jean par la main et le conduisant vers le talus, lui dit :

— Monte...

« Le plancher de l'avion est solide et tu ne pèses pas lourd. Tu n'as pas peur.

— Non, mais où allons-nous ?

— Tu verras...

Jean s'installe parmi les perdreaux qui lui font place avec beaucoup d'empressement. Chacun tient le bout d'une baguette dans son bec et Jean est assis au milieu de toutes les baguettes rassemblées.

Le lièvre prend place devant Jean et donne un coup de sifflet. Les perdreaux battent des ailes....

Alors Jean se sent léger, léger. Le vent souffle plus fort... Jean monte sur la route des hérons, des alouettes et des canards.

QUAND on fut à une certaine hauteur, Jean qui avait tenu le nez en l'air pendant qu'on montait le baissa...

Il cherche des perdreaux et découvre des panneaux de monoplan, il ne voit plus de branchettes, mais un fuselage et s'aperçoit qu'il n'est plus assis sur de fragiles brindilles, mais dans une carlingue fermée.

Devant lui, ce n'est plus un lièvre, mais un pilote en pelisse fauve sous un bonnet de cuir, attentif aux commandes et aux bruits de son moteur, fixant la carte et la boussole.

Jean songe aussitôt qu'il doit s'agir là d'une de ces histoires comme celles que sa maman lui a racontées jadis, où les citrouilles deviennent carrosses et les lézards laquais en livrée.

C'était très beau dans le ciel... Ceux qui savent compter auraient pu compter les étoiles ; mais ça aurait été trop long. La lune était beaucoup plus grosse. Un œil énorme avec des taches...

Jean découvrait au fond de la nuit des choses bien étonnantes... Une longue traînée blanche comme une robe de mariée avec toutes sortes de paillettes.

Des étoiles rouges, d'autres vertes, d'autres bleues ; certaines avaient l'air de se tenir par des mains invisibles pour former des rondes, des figures, des dessins...

De temps en temps, une ou deux se détachaient des autres, en filant, pour danser ailleurs... Quelques-unes, toutes seules, orgueilleuses, luisaient à part, comme vexées de la clarté vulgaire que dépensait cette grosse lanterne de lune...

Mais, soudain, voilà que la lune semble pâlir... Une lueur rouge monte de la terre et baigne l'avion. On descend à toute vitesse vers des lumières. Jean ferme les yeux parce que ça va décidément trop vite.

Quand il les rouvre, il se trouve assis sur son derrière au milieu d'un toit plat, avec autour de lui vingt perdreaux qui picorent et un lièvre qui gambade.

Jean se met sur ses pieds, il regarde et il écoute.

Si tu avais entendu ce bruit !

Autour de lui, c'était des sifflets de locomotives et des fuites de vapeur et des ronflements de machines et des explosions de moteurs.

Dans la nuit rouge flambaient les cheminées des fourneaux où l'on fond l'acier. D'immenses maisons de terre et de fer semblaient brûler... Par terre des rails luisaient, se croisaient et s'entortillaient comme des couleuvres sous des milliers de lampes électriques.

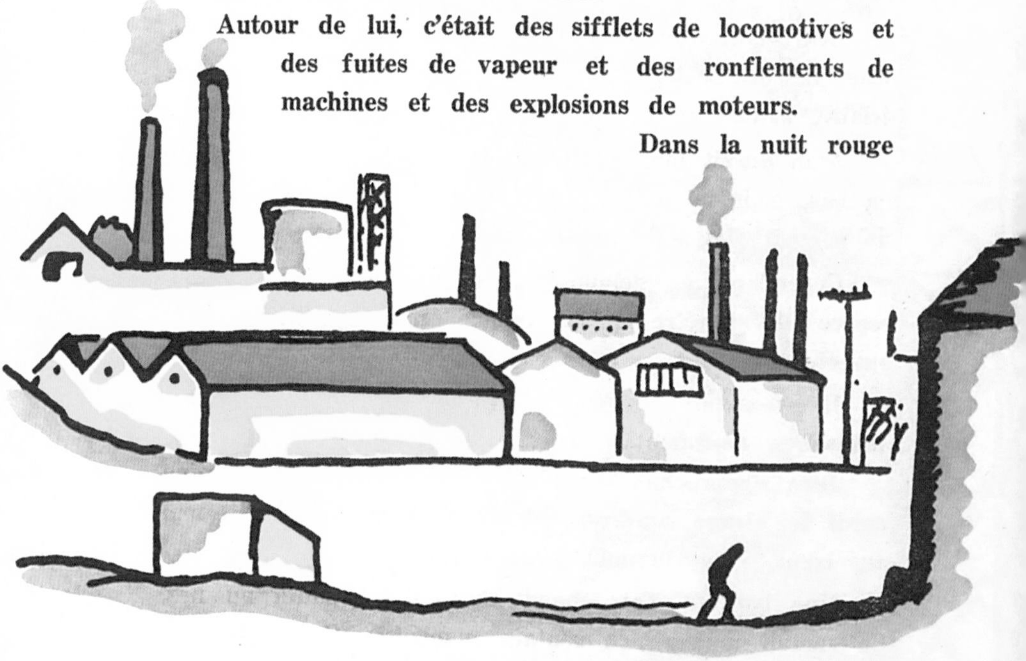

Les wagonnets succédaient aux wagonnets, les wagons aux wagons, les locomotives aux locomotives. De longs trains noirs entraient dans les campagnes en soufflant et en crachant, et des camions roulaient sur les pavés des cours, comme des éléphants en fer.

Sous les pieds de Jean il y avait un toit de verre éclairé par en dessous, et ce toit vibrait tellement que ça lui chatouillait la plante des pieds.

Les perdreaux voletaient comme s'ils eussent eu peur de se brûler les pattes et le lièvre, le ventre éclairé, avait l'air d'avoir mis un gilet blanc.

Jean aurait bien voulu savoir ce qu'il pouvait y avoir en bas, mais le verre du toit était peint en gris et l'on ne pouvait rien voir à travers.

Cependant, à quelques pas de là, une trappe, une espèce de fenêtre qu'on appelle une tabatière, était ouverte.

Il en sortait un grand rayon de lumière, où des poussières dansaient...

Jean s'approcha et voulut regarder. Mais à peine eut-il le visage au-dessus du trou qu'il se sentit mal au cœur, mais tu sais, tout à fait mal au cœur.

Une bouffée d'air chaud et fade lui sauta au nez. Ça sentait mauvais, ça sentait mauvais... Ça sentait la sueur, la crasse, l'huile brûlée, le chien mouillé, le cuir cuit, et toutes les plus détestables odeurs que tu pourras imaginer, mais concentrées.

— Fais un effort, petit Jean... C'est dans cet air-là que doivent vivre des millions d'hommes comme toi...

— Et qu'est-ce qu'ils ont fait de méchant pour ça..?

— Rien, ils sont pauvres... C'est là-dedans que ta maman et tant d'autres mamans ont pris mal.

Jean pince son nez avec une main, met l'autre devant sa bouche, et regarde.

D'abord il ne voit qu'une buée bleue... Puis il distingue des courroies, enfin il aperçoit des machines, des centaines de machines, des mécaniques qui tapent, perçent, coupent, tournent, roulent, aplatissent, amincissent, vont, viennent, glissent, grinçent, sous les lumières.

— C'est l'Usine, dit Jean.

Et comme il savait que les machines ne marchaient pas toutes seules, il se mit à chercher ceux qui les faisaient marcher.

Il n'était pas facile de les voir. Ils étaient si luisants de sueur, si couverts de poussière, si gris, qu'ils se confondaient d'abord avec les machines. On aurait dit que c'était les machines qui les faisaient marcher, comme ces pantins qui font toujours les mêmes mouvements quand on tire sur leurs ficelles. Jean essaya de les compter avec ses doigts, mais il ne savait pas compter plus loin que cinq, et tout ce qu'il pouvait dire, c'est qu'ils étaient « beaucoup de fois cinq. »

Comme le travail l'intéressait, il chercha quelqu'un qu'il pût regarder travailler... Quand il eut choisi, il ne sut pas très bien si c'était un homme ou une femme.

C'était un être pâle, vêtu d'une grande blouse bleue et coiffé d'un serre-tête. Il toussait du fond du dos, et de temps en temps, en se cachant, il essuyait sa bouche avec son mouchoir. Il travaillait sous une énorme courroie en mouvement. Et le vent que faisait la courroie soulevait parfois un pan de son bonnet...

Jean avait choisi cette personne-là parce qu'elle ressemblait un peu à son papa et parce qu'elle toussait comme sa maman...

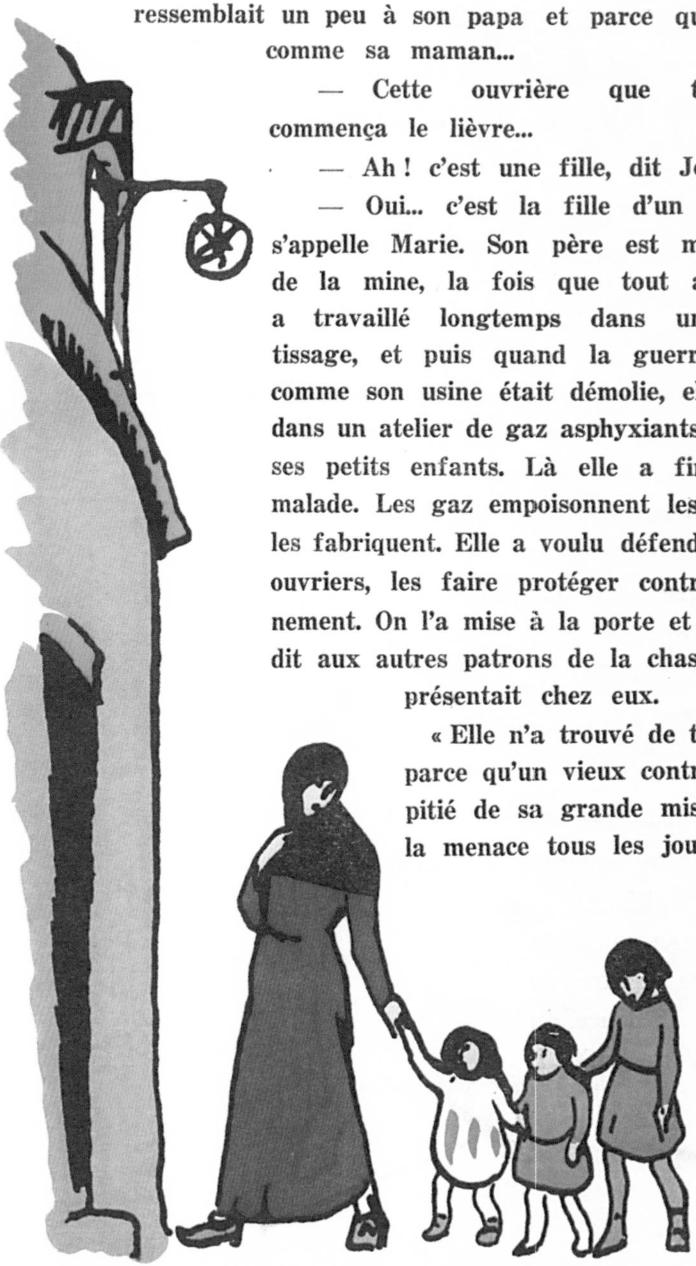

— Cette ouvrière que tu regardes, commença le lièvre...

— Ah ! c'est une fille, dit Jean.

— Oui... c'est la fille d'un mineur. Elle s'appelle Marie. Son père est mort au fond de la mine, la fois que tout a sauté. Elle a travaillé longtemps dans une usine de tissage, et puis quand la guerre est venue, comme son usine était démolie, elle est entrée dans un atelier de gaz asphyxiants pour nourrir ses petits enfants. Là elle a fini de tomber malade. Les gaz empoisonnent les ouvriers qui les fabriquent. Elle a voulu défendre les autres ouvriers, les faire protéger contre l'empoisonnement. On l'a mise à la porte et son patron a dit aux autres patrons de la chasser si elle se présentait chez eux.

« Elle n'a trouvé de travail ici que parce qu'un vieux contremaître a eu pitié de sa grande misère. Mais on la menace tous les jours...

« Et vois-tu, Jean, elle a trois petites, petites filles, dont le papa est à la guerre.

Et tous ceux et toutes celles qui travaillent autour d'elles sont pauvres comme elle et travaillent comme elle de longs jours et de longues nuits jusqu'à ce qu'ils tombent...

« Et quand ils sont bien vieux, on les jette dehors, sans toit et sans pain...

Jean aurait voulu descendre au milieu de l'atelier, embrasser Marie, si pauvre, si bonne et si malade, embrasser aussi les autres et leur parler de sa maman...

Soudain il entendit un cri qui perça le bruit régulier des machines et il vit Marie arrachée du sol et emportée par la grosse courroie, retomber par terre comme une loque, brisée. Elle ne bougeait plus.

Jean recula...

— Allons-nous-en ! allons-nous-en, lièvre ! dit-il... Tu m'as trompé quand tu m'as dit que tu me ferais rire. On fait trop de mal ici aux papas et aux mamans... Je ne veux pas rester ici... allons-nous-en...

— C'est pourtant la vie qui attend les enfants pauvres, dit le lièvre.

Alors Jean-sans-Pain serra sa tête contre la poitrine tiède et douce du lièvre et là, se mit à sangloter.

QUE lui arriva-t-il ? Comment l'avion repartit-il ? Comment l'atterrissage se fit-il ? Jean avait trop de chagrin pour y penser, et tu l'imagineras toi-même, si tu veux.

Ce qu'il y a de sûr, c'est que Jean-sans-Pain se retrouva soudain au milieu d'une maison splendide. C'était beau ! C'était beau ! Ou plutôt non. C'était doré ! C'était doré !

Au plafond il y avait des dames bleues et roses qui volaient entre de petits amours qui portaient des bouquets de fleurs.

En bas, il y avait des fleurs partout et de petites tables couvertes de nappes bien blanches, bien raides et surchargées d'or, d'argent, de cristaux et de vaisselles si transparentes qu'on aurait pu voir le jour au travers...

Il n'y a que de très rares petits garçons et de très rares petites filles qui aient vu ces choses. D'abord, parce qu'il en est très peu qui soient assez riches pour les voir et aussi parce que les gens très riches ont honte d'emmener dans ces endroits-là leurs petits enfants. Ils y vont seuls, pour cacher leur épouvantable gourmandise.

Derrière chaque table, il y avait un monsieur en noir et en blanc qui donnait des choses à manger, en faisant des révérences.

Il y avait là des pâtés, de beaux pâtés croustillants et brillants.

Il y avait des poulardes truffées, dorées de la tête au derrière et des rôtis de toutes les viandes.

Il y avait des poissons de toute espèce, de la baleine jusqu'aux poissons rouges.

Il y avait des glaces à la fraise, à la framboise, à la pèche, à la pistache, à l'abricot, à la vanille et à la rose.

Il y avait des crèmes au chocolat.

Il y avait des gâteaux de tous les noms et de tous les pays, des éclairs, des choux, des feuilletés, des madeleines, des tartes, des soufflés, des sablés, des chaussons, des quatre quarts, des frangipanes, des pains d'épices, des nonnettes, des farinettes, des puits d'amour, des beignets et des babas.

Il y avait de petites maisons en nougat et des pyramides de confitures.

Il y avait des fruits de toutes les saisons.

Il y avait même un ragoût noir, appelé civet, qui faisait une très mauvaise impression au lièvre.

Mais ce qui remplissait Jean-sans-Pain d'admiration, c'était le pain.

Il y avait du pain blanc en flûtes, mais tu sais, si blanc qu'il ne pouvait pas y avoir de gâteaux plus blancs, du pain qui sentait bon, qui croquait et qui fondait.

Le nez de Jean s'allongeait.

Et ça brillait, et ça brillait !

D'abord il y avait les lampes qui brillaient, et puis il y avait les lustres, et puis il y avait les glaces des murs, et puis il y avait les carafes, et puis il y avait les dames qui semblaient vouloir briller plus que les carafes tellement elles étaient couvertes de diamants.

Les messieurs aussi brillaient, les uns par leur monocle, les autres par leur crâne chauve, certains par leurs chemises, tous par leurs bagues de toutes les couleurs.

Il y avait là des officiers de tous les pays, avec des galons, des croix et des décorations étalées sur leur poitrine comme des batteries de cuisine attachées à des jarretelles rouges, vertes, bleues ou jaunes.

On aurait dit qu'ils avaient envie de marcher sur les pieds de tout le monde.

Et tous ceux et toutes celles qui étaient là, devant les tables, ressemblaient aux plus vilaines ou aux plus bêtes de toutes les bêtes, sous leurs bijoux et leurs beaux habits.

Il y avait un monsieur rose et chauve, avec un cou gras qui lui rentrait dans les épaules, un monsieur avec de grosses lèvres, un gros nez rond, et de petits yeux perdus dans la graisse, un monsieur qui ressemblait tout à fait à un cochon fatigué.

Il y avait un autre monsieur, maigre, avec une longue figure jaune sous une pointe de cheveux en brosse, un long nez qui portait un lorgnon, une lèvre tombante, des yeux trop hauts, et des oreilles pointues. Tu aurais juré que c'était un âne.

Il y avait encore une espèce d'homme en robe violette, avec de gros yeux ronds qui lui sortaient du front, une bouche énorme fendue jusqu'aux oreilles, et un menton qui se perdait dans sa ceinture. Il ouvrait tout le temps la bouche comme un crapaud qui a trop chaud.

Il y avait un général en grand costume, gros à faire craquer toutes les chaises, un général avec une épaisse figure rouge sous des sourcils inégaux, énormes et blancs, un général avec une épaisse moustache jaunâtre... Il avait l'air de dormir tout le temps, mais il ne dormait pas, il était occupé à digérer tout ce qu'il avait mangé... Tu aurais cru que c'était le Bœuf gras...

Et il y avait aussi des tas de gens, des dames qui ressemblaient à des oies, à des chèvres, à des girafes et à des lézards, des messieurs qui ressemblaient à des singes, à des dindons, à des boucs, à des tigres, à des crocodiles, à des loups. Et ça mangeait, et ça buvait, et ça riait ! Fallait voir !

Jean, le lièvre et les perdreaux s'étaient réfugiés sous une table où personne ne mangeait et ils regardaient par-dessous la nappe...

— Faut-il qu'ils travaillent dans leurs usines pour pouvoir arriver à manger comme ça, dit Jean avec admiration.

— C'est ce qui te trompe, Jean !

— Comment ?

— C'est parce qu'ils ne travaillent pas qu'ils mangent comme ça.

— Ah ! Alors, comment font-ils ? Ils trichent ?

— Oui, ils trichent, c'est-à-dire, ils volent.

— C'est bien vilain...

— Vois-tu, par exemple ce monsieur qui ressemble si terriblement à un gros cochon fatigué, dit le lièvre, le vois-tu avec son ruban rouge à la boutonnière et son gros cigare ?

— Oui.

— C'est le patron de Marie, tu sais Marie, de l'usine...

— Oh ! alors, il faut vite le prévenir. Il va prendre son aéroplane ou son automobile et aller dans l'atelier pour s'occuper d'elle...

— Si tu savais comme tu perdrais ton temps ! Il ne la connait même pas, et s'il l'avait connue, il l'aurait renvoyée...

— Oh ! dit Jean indigné, c'est un méchant alors.

— Non... c'est un patron...

— Ah ! Est-ce que c'est la même chose ?

Le lièvre ne répondit pas.

— Vois-tu, continua-t-il, ce général qui ressemble au Boeuf gras, et qui est en train de dormir sous ses décorations, c'est lui qui conduit la guerre.

— Mais, c'est pas ici la guerre. C'est sur le front...

— Pour lui, c'est ici, la guerre, il ne se bat jamais, mais il fait battre les autres à sa place. Lui, il mange et il dort.

— Alors, il triche aussi.

— Il a comme ça fait tuer beaucoup de papas...

— Ah ? Mais c'est un méchant aussi ?

— Non... c'est un général.

« Et celui-là qui a une robe violette et une grande ceinture, celui-là qui ressemble à un grand crapaud, c'est un évêque. Sa religion l'oblige à être pauvre et à aimer tous les hommes, mais celui-là commande aux soldats de tuer leurs frères et il est très riche.

— Tricheur ! sale tricheur ! souffla Jean qui commençait à se mettre en colère...

— Et celui-là qui a l'air d'un âne, tu le vois ?

— Oui.

— C'est un ministre.

Jean aurait bien demandé au lièvre d'autres explications, s'il ne s'était passé à ce moment précis quelque chose d'extraordinaire...

Patatras ! Boum !

Le général venait de rouler sous la table.

Il avait tellement, tellement mangé et tellement bu, que la chaise avait décidé de ne pas le porter plus longtemps. Elle s'était cassée.

Crac !

Et le général était tombé par terre, entraînant avec lui la nappe, les fourchettes, les assiettes, les bouteilles, et un plat de crème qui s'était étalé en plein sur son ventre énorme.

Comme on se précipitait de tous les côtés pour aller au secours du grand militaire qui n'était pas capable de se relever tout seul, Jean sortit de dessous la nappe et, s'adressant à l'un des messieurs en habit noir qui servaient, demanda gentiment et sans rire :

— Est-ce qu'il s'est fait mal, le tricheur ?

Pour toute réponse et avant même qu'il ait pu faire un mouvement, Jean-sans-Pain recevait une énorme gifle qui l'envoyait rouler à dix pas. A peine avait-il eu le temps de se relever qu'il voyait arriver sur lui des tas de messieurs en habit noir, des officiers avec des sabres, des dames avec des ongles en avant. Et tous criaient :

— Arrêtez-le ! c'est lui ! c'est le mendiant qui a fait tomber notre général. Arrêtez-le ! Allez chercher les sergents de ville !

A ces mots, Jean-sans-Pain se croit perdu. Il empoigne à tout hasard le lièvre par la peau du cou.

— Tiens bien ! dit le lièvre, et le voilà qui part en galopant, entraînant Jean dans sa course folle.

Les perdreaux pendant ce temps-là s'envolent avec un bruit terrible et font éclater les lampes électriques qu'ils rencontrent.

Vrrrrrrou ! Pan ! Pan !

Les officiers croient que c'est un bombardement qui commence et ils se réfugient courageusement sous les tables. Des dames s'évanouissent. Les perdreaux suivent Jean et le lièvre, donnant de temps en temps de grands coups d'aile et de durs coups de bec dans la figure de ceux qui veulent les rattraper.

— Katchouic ! et je te pique ! Katchouic ! et je te fouette !

Et Jean court, et il court, et il court...

Tantôt il est sur ses pieds, tantôt il est sur son ventre, tantôt il est sur son derrière, tantôt il est à cheval sur le dos du lièvre.

Il saute dans un couloir, grimpe un escalier, en descend un autre, traverse les cuisines, où les marmitons effrayés renversent les sauces et plongent dans les marmites, trouve enfin la porte, poursuivi toujours par les mêmes gens enragés qui s'élancent dans la rue derrière lui.

Mais, à peine est-il dehors, que tous les perdreaux se rassemblent autour de lui et devant la foule furieuse et stupéfaite des dames, des messieurs en noir, des officiers et des sergents de ville, emportent notre Jean et son lièvre dans le clair de lune.

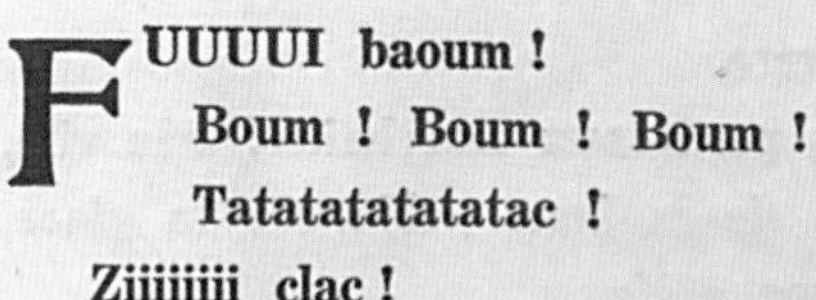

FUUUUI baoum !
Boum ! Boum ! Boum !
Tatatatatatatac !
Ziiiiiii clac !
Rrrrraou ! Rrrrraou !

La terre sautait.

On était à la guerre maintenant, et en plein, tu sais.

Il faisait un froid épouvantable et Jean-sans-Pain claquait les dents en grelottant au milieu des bruits effrayants.

Sa joue giflée le brûlait, mais il n'y pensait guère, tant ce qu'il voyait était laid.

C'est très laid la guerre.

Jean, le lièvre et les perdreaux marchaient très vite, sautant de trou en trou, de la boue gelée sur la glace, et de la glace sur la boue gelée.

Jean tombait tout le temps. Sur les champs de bataille on tombe tout le temps parce qu'il y a toutes sortes de choses qui vous attrapent par les pieds.

— Qu'est-ce que c'est que ce sale petit garçon qui ose venir ici ? disait dans sa barbe le fil de fer barbelé.

Et vlan ! il s'entortillait autour de la jambe de Jean.

— D'où vient-il ce marmot ? disait la glace qui s'était formée sur l'eau des trous. Je le mangerais bien volontiers car il doit être tendre.

Et croc ! la glace s'ouvrait sous les pieds de Jean.

— Tiens, tiens, voilà un moucheron que je transformerais bien volontiers en bouillie pour les corbeaux, disait le gros obus furieux de ne pas avoir éclaté. Si seulement il pouvait me taper dessus au bon endroit !

Et bing ! il se mettait sur la route de Jean.

— Ah ! ah ! disait la baïonnette. Y a bon, voilà de jolis petits pieds avec des souliers percés. Je m'en vais les faire saigner !

Et pic ! la baïonnette s'enfonçait dans la semelle de Jean.

Jean, à force de trébucher sur les obus, de tomber dans les fils de fer, de se piquer les pieds aux baïonnettes, et de s'enfoncer dans la glace, commençait à avoir une forte envie de s'en aller. Seulement il n'osait pas le dire.

Il avait le nez qui saignait, les mains écorchées, les pieds trempés et déchirés, le tablier en lambeaux, le pantalon jaune tout percé, mais le lièvre et les perdreaux marchaient toujours et Jean ne voulait pas les perdre.

— C'est encore long, la guerre ? demandait Jean.

— Oui, ça dure des lieues et des lieues, des années et des années, répondait le lièvre.

Et la marche continuait.

Parfois des fusées montaient dans le

ciel et tout devenait blanc, comme si on avait versé de la farine sur le monde. A ce moment-là il fallait se coucher tout de suite, n'importe où. Sur la glace ou dans les fils de fer pointus. Et les balles sifflaient de tous les côtés cherchant à mordre.

— Fuuuui ! Où est-il ?

— Ziiiiiiii ! Je le cherche !

— Fuifuifuifuifui ! En l'air peut-être !

— Tac ! Manqué !

— Ziiou ! Flof ! J'ai tapé par terre !

— Tactactactactac ! On ne passe pas !

La fusée s'éteignait et l'on repartait.

On traversait des ponts, au-dessus de longs fossés noirs et puants où rien ne paraissait pouvoir vivre.

— Les tranchées, disait le lièvre.

Puis c'était encore des fils de fer, des trous, des bosses...

A un endroit Jean s'arrêta. Il y avait là beaucoup d'hommes, les uns couchés, les autres à genoux. L'un de ceux-là avait l'air d'arranger des fils de fer.

— C'est l'ennemi ? demanda Jean, tout bas, au lièvre.

— Non.

— Ah !

Jean s'approcha de celui qui était dans les fils de fer. Quand il fut tout près, il attendit. L'homme ne

remuait pas. Jean n'osait pas l'appeler. Une fusée monta. Jean ouvrit les yeux tant qu'il put. L'homme avait les lèvres qui grimaçaient, un petit trou noir au milieu du front et une grande figure toute verte.

Jean poussa un cri, fit un saut en arrière et se laissa dégringoler dans un trou d'obus où les perdreaux et le lièvre le ramassèrent. Il était tout pâle sous ses écorchures rouges, et tout glacé sous ses vêtements déchirés.

— Qui c'est, dit-il, celui-là, là haut ?

— C'est un papa qu'une de ces petites balles que tu entends siffler a tapé dans la tête. Il serait devenu un grand savant plus tard.

— Mais alors, pourquoi était-il là ?

— Parce que le gros général qui mange tant lui avait commandé d'être là.

— Le tricheur ?

— Oui.

Jean se mit à grelotter plus fort. Alors les perdreaux se serrèrent tout autour de lui. Ils montèrent sur son cou, sur sa poitrine, sur son ventre, sur ses jambes et ouvrirent leurs petites ailes pour lui faire une bonne couverture de plumes, tandis que le lièvre se glissait derrière sa tête, comme un oreiller bien chaud et bien doux.

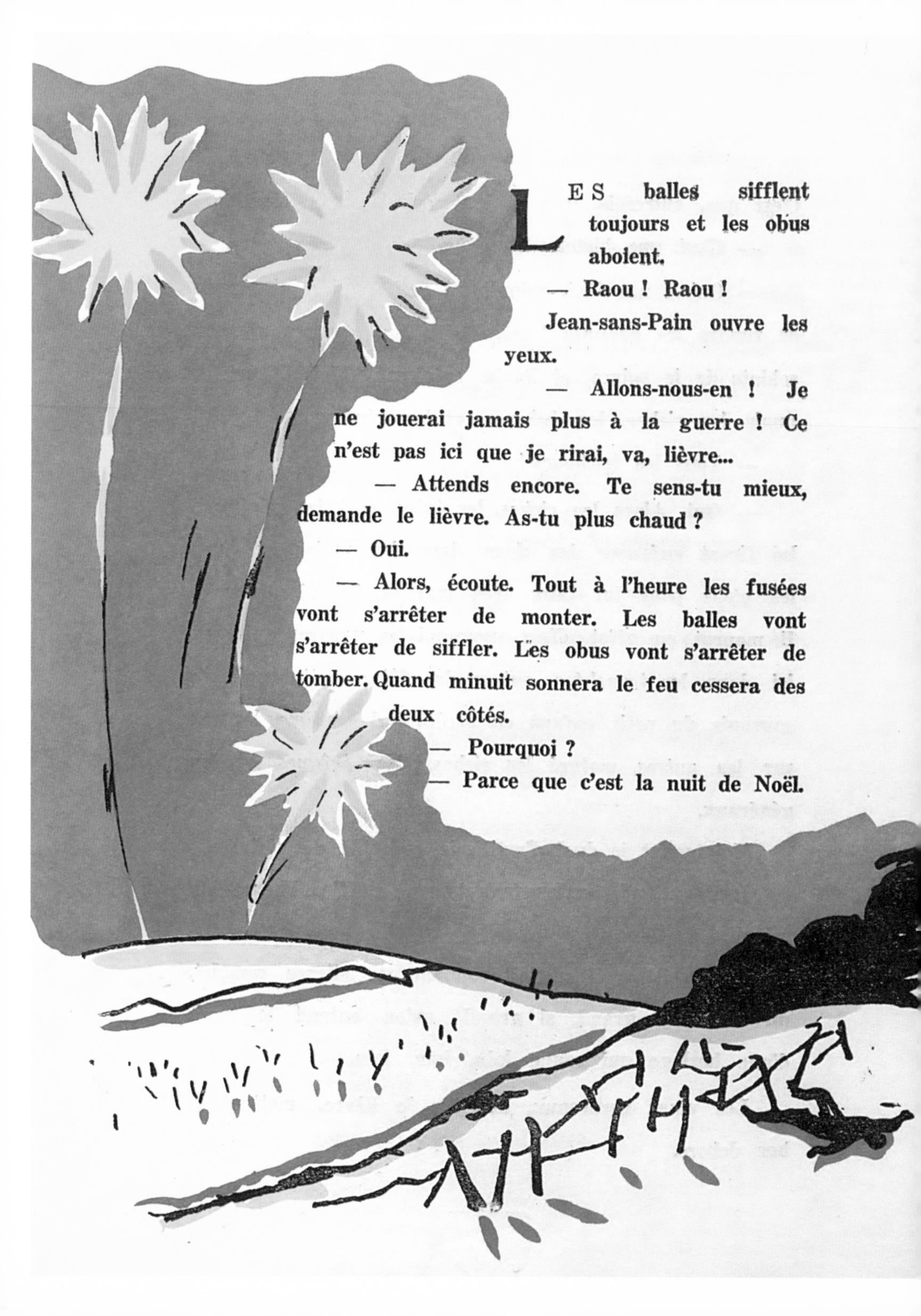

LES balles sifflent toujours et les obus aboient.

— Raou ! Raou !

Jean-sans-Pain ouvre les yeux.

— Allons-nous-en ! Je ne jouerai jamais plus à la guerre ! Ce n'est pas ici que je rirai, va, lièvre...

— Attends encore. Te sens-tu mieux, demande le lièvre. As-tu plus chaud ?

— Oui.

— Alors, écoute. Tout à l'heure les fusées vont s'arrêter de monter. Les balles vont s'arrêter de siffler. Les obus vont s'arrêter de tomber. Quand minuit sonnera le feu cessera des deux côtés.

— Pourquoi ?

— Parce que c'est la nuit de Noël.

C'est que, autrefois, il y a des siècles et des siècles...

— C'est une histoire ?

— Oui..... naquit à minuit un petit garçon. Il essaya de rendre les hommes bons, il dit aux pauvres et aux soldats de le suivre, et ils le suivirent. Mais il voulut punir les riches, les évêques, et les généraux.

— Tous les tricheurs !

— Oui. Alors les riches, les évêques et les généraux lui firent enfoncer des clous dans les mains et dans les pieds pour lui faire très mal et le faire mourir. Il mourut en effet. C'est pourquoi les pauvres qui sont ici dans les tranchées, ont voulu fêter cette nuit le souvenir du petit enfant en arrêtant de se tirer les uns sur les autres, malgré les riches, les évêques et les généraux.

Maintenant le duel d'artillerie redouble de violence.

Jean attend, en retenant son souffle, l'heure de minuit.

Mais voilà qu'il se fait soudain un silence complet, un silence si grand, si grand, qu'on entend le bruit d'une horloge qui sonne loin, loin, loin.

Les vingt perdreaux, derrière le lièvre, mettent le bec dehors.

— Tu peux venir, Jean, dit le lièvre.

Jean grimpe et sort de l'entonnoir. Le voilà sur un tas de terre blanche, debout. La lune est dans son plein. Jean regarde à droite et à gauche. Il ne voit que la terre gelée avec des lignes grises qui se perdent dans la nuit.

Mais, il lui semble bien, en regardant mieux que quelque chose bouge à droite. A gauche aussi... A droite, ça a bien remué. La lune frappe un visage blanc, sous un casque, et la moitié d'un homme sort de la tranchée. Puis d'autres têtes, et d'autres casques, et des bérets. A gauche, timides, des formes noires apparaissent. Des casques aussi, des calots. Soudain, des deux côtés, il semble à Jean qu'une chanson monte...

— Camarades ! Camarades ! Camarades !

Et puis le silence. Maintenant les hommes sont sur les parapets, sans armes. Ils se regardent. C'est la première fois qu'ils se voient. Jean se demande ce qu'ils vont faire.

Les hommes se tendent les bras.

Jean est debout entre les lignes. Les soldats ne l'ont peut-être pas vu encore.

Mais lui, soudain, se sent heureux, heureux... Ses petites lèvres gercées s'entr'ouvrent. Des fossettes apparaissent dans ses joues écorchées. Et voilà que Jean se met à sourire.

Jean-sans-Pain sourit.

C'est la première fois de sa vie qu'il sourit. Et ce

sourire met tant de lumière sur son visage, et ses yeux brillent si fort et ses cheveux prennent tellement de rayons à la lune, qu'une grande clarté se répand autour de lui.

— Regardez ! regardez !

Les soldats s'avancent, émerveillés, des deux côtés à la fois. Ils arrivent près de Jean, en rampant sous les fils de fer. Ils s'agenouillent devant lui. Ils embrassent ses petites mains, sa petite bague en aluminium, son tablier déchiré, ses pieds qui saignent. Ils ne font de mal ni au lièvre, ni aux perdreaux. Tout au contraire, ils les saluent bien poliment.

Jean dit aux soldats :

— Pourquoi vous agenouillez-vous ?

Et eux répondent :

— Parce que tu es « l'Enfant qui doit venir » !

— Non, je suis Jean-sans-Pain. Mon papa n'est pas revenu de la guerre. Ma maman avait beaucoup de mal hier, et j'ai dix ans.

Les hommes se relèvent et veulent embrasser Jean. Ils lui montrent les photographies de leurs petits garçons, de leurs petites filles, de leurs fiancées, de leurs mamans. C'est si bon de trouver un petit enfant qui sourit, sur un champ de bataille. Et chacun voudrait raconter son histoire.

— Moi, je suis Heinrich-le-pauvre, et je suis né à Munich, en Allemagne, dit l'un des soldats en ôtant son gros casque. J'ai une petite fille qui m'attend en brodant des fleurs, et qui ne me reverra peut-être jamais...

— Moi, je suis Henri-le-Malheureux et je suis né près de Paris, en France, dit un autre. J'ai une vieille maman qui m'attend en pleurant, et je ne lui reviendrai peut-être jamais...

— Pourquoi ? demande Jean, qui voudrait bien rendre Heinrich à sa petite fille et Henri à sa vieille maman.

— Parce qu'on nous fera du mal.

— Qui ça ? qui te fera du mal, Heinrich ?

Heinrich-le-pauvre montre avec son doigt Henri-le-Malheureux.

— Et qui te fera du mal à toi, Henri ?

Henri-le-Malheureux montre avec son doigt Heinrich-le-pauvre.

— Vous êtes donc bien méchants tous les deux ? demande Jean.

— Oh ! non, disent en même temps Henri et Heinrich. Nous nous aimons bien au contraire. Nous nous apportions cette nuit de petits cadeaux en signe d'amitié...

Et Jean voit Henri qui sort de sa poche un gros morceau de pain, tandis que Heinrich tend à Henri un beau paquet de tabac.

— Alors ? dit Jean, je ne comprends plus. Ce que je vois, c'est que vous êtes bons tous les deux.

« Mais alors, alors ?

Un murmure sourd et triste parcourt les rangs des soldats.

— C'est la guerre ...

— Mais pourquoi c'est la guerre ? demande Jean.

Personne ne répond. Les soldats baissent la tête et n'osent plus se regarder...

Mais voilà que Jean revoit la machine qui a brisé Marie, les ouvriers travaillant dans l'air qui sent mauvais, le patron gros comme un cochon, l'évêque bâillant comme un crapaud, le ministre sot comme un âne, le général qui ressemble au Bœuf gras, et l'affreux, l'horrible champ de bataille.

Et comme les soldats se taisent toujours...

— Mais si tous les pauvres et tous les soldats du monde s'entendaient comme ce soir ? demande Jean.

— Alors ça changerait.... disent les soldats.

— Quand je serai grand, il faudra que ça change ! s'écrie Jean-sans-Pain. Gare, les tricheurs !

Et il ferme ses petits poings.

Les soldats étaient tout à fait étonnés d'entendre un si petit garçon dire des choses aussi sages. Ils s'embrassaient entre eux et se faisaient des présents. Il

y en avait qui criaient « A bas la guerre ! » et d'autres « Révolution ! » On pleurait, on riait, on parlait des mamans, des femmes et des enfants. Il n'y avait plus de « Boches » ni de « Franzous ». Il n'y avait que des frères.

Les poches de Jean étaient bourrées de chocolat et de pain de soldat. Il y avait même une toute petite boîte de confitures de fraises.

Jean - sans - Pain riait, maintenant.

La lune aussi riait, de bonheur.

Les fils de fer rentraient sous terre, dégoûtés.

Les vieux obus rouillés s'enfonçaient dans la boue.

Les baïonnettes se cassaient.

Les canons se couchaient sur le dos.

Les fusils brisaient leurs crosses.

Les drapeaux tricolores se déchiraient.

Les perdreaux faisaient une ronde en chantant, et le lièvre dansait au milieu, tantôt sur les pattes de devant, tantôt sur les pattes de derrière.

TU me demandes maintenant ce que Jean devient, et ce que devient le lièvre et ce que deviennent les perdreaux, et ce que deviennent les soldats, et ce que deviennent les tricheurs ? Les tricheurs seront punis. Mais cela, c'est pour une autre histoire...

Sache seulement pour cette fois-ci, que le lièvre fit venir des aéroplanes pour tout le monde et que tous les soldats, chacun installé sur un bon monoplan qui faisait 350 kilomètres à l'heure, s'envolèrent vers le pays de l'Est, où tous les hommes apprennent à être libres et à être bons.

Qui ne travaille pas
ne doit pas manger.

Cet album a été imprimé
pour le compte
des Editions "CLARTÉ"
par la Grande Imprimerie Perfecta
8, Rue Neuve-Popincourt,
Paris (11e)

L'enluminure et la reliure
ont été exécutées par
la Coopérative Ouvrière "Photo-Coloris"
76, Boulevard Voltaire,
Paris (11e)

Afterword

Paul Vaillant-Couturier's "War" against War

During World War I, at Christmas time in 1914, there were sudden, widespread unofficial ceasefires along the Eastern Front organized by the French, British, and German soldiers. They crossed trenches to exchange food, souvenirs, and ideas. In some cases, they played soccer, sang Christmas carols, held burial ceremonies, and exchanged prisoners of war. The ceasefires were also held at various places in 1915. However, by 1916, the so-called "Great War" had become more bitter and divisive, and the officers in the French, British, and German armies squashed the ceasefires. Killing was much more important than peacemaking.

Paul Vaillant-Couturier (1892-1937) was one of the French soldiers among those who celebrated truce. As a young man from a well-to-do bourgeois family in Paris, he had never thought he would one day fight for France and kill Germans. His parents were successful singers, actors, and artists, and as he indicated in his fictional autobiography, *The French* Boy (1931), he was groomed to become a professional lawyer or engineer. An exceptional student, he attended one of the best lycées in Paris and later enrolled at the Sorbonne. At the same time, he wrote poems and plays and was regarded as a kind of Bohemian artist. Though he eventually became a lawyer, he did not practice much. Instead, he followed in his parents' footsteps and became an artist. In 1912 and 1913 he wrote plays and poems, painted, and published essays in an anarchistic journal. He did not take politics very seriously and led a "Bohemian" carefree life until he enlisted in the French army in 1913.

From 1914 to 1916, Vaillant-Couturier served in the infantry and participated in the brutal war of the trenches. It was during this time that he began writing critical articles about the war for various newspapers. It was clear from his viewpoint that he had become much more of a socialist and pacifist than a "Bohemian artist." He had come to realize that thousands of young French men and women were considered insignificant creatures or tools, whose basic value was to protect and serve the interests of the ruling classes. After being wounded in 1916, he did not leave the army because he was dedicated to the troops with whom he was serving. So, he joined the artillery corps as a lieutenant in 1917 and almost died from a gas attack in 1918. Despite his injuries, he kept opposing and exposing the contradictory policies of the generals and officers in various newspapers and magazines. Consequently he was sentenced to thirty days in prison for being too outspoken about warmongers. By the time he was belatedly discharged from the army in 1919, he decided to abandon his career as an artist and to devote himself to politics, namely to bring about greater social justice and democracy in France. This did not mean that he stopped writing altogether. In particular, he wrote about his experiences in the war in *La Guere des soldats* (The War of Soldiers, 1919) and *Lettres à mes amis* (Letters to My Friends, 1920), and he continued writing poems. His major contribution to European culture at that time, however, was his book for children *Jean sans Pain* (*Johnny* Breadless, 1921), illustrated by the talented Jean Picart le Doux, who shared his political views. Vaillant-Couturier did not believe in mincing his words or lying to children, and this extraordinary revolutionary book, a pacifist fairy tale, was to have an influence on writers in France and Germany as it paved the way for many progressive books for children.

Due to his popularity as a journalist and his service during the war, Vaillant-Couturier was elected as a deputy representing the district in which he was living in Paris, and in 1920, he became one of the founders of the newly formed Communist Party. Thanks to his interventions, especially his critique of fascism and the exploitation of French workers, he was re-elected as a deputy in 1924. Once he moved to the suburb of Villejuif, which, at that time, was a working-class district, Vaillant-Couturier assumed the position of editor of the daily communist newspaper *L'Humanité*. Known for his integrity and skill as an orator, Vaillant-Couturier spent the 1920s developing the newspaper and strengthening the Communist Party, even though he often disagreed with its policies. His major aim, aside from representing the people in his district, was to further an international cultural movement that would contribute to a more humane and just society. After he resigned as editor of *L'Humanité* in 1929 because of political differences, Vaillant-Couturier did not abandon his commitment to communism, and in the 1930s, he kept writing and giving talks against fascism and played an important role in the movement to form a Front Populaire of workers, farmers, and the middle class against the Nazis and other right-wing parties in Europe.

In 1933 he returned to *L'Humanité* as editor and continued writing political articles, pamphlets, plays, and poetry in support of efforts by European writers to form a socialist federation. At the same time, Vaillant-Couturier did not forget his commitment to write books for children. One of his most insightful books was *Le Malheur d'etre jeune* (The Misfortune of Being Young, 1933), which depicted the unenviable situation of young people in France during the 1930s:

> Before the war, to be young meant to have a full life ahead of oneself.
> During the war, to be young meant to have death ahead of oneself.
> Today, to be young means to have a miserable life ahead of oneself.
> Certain older people keep telling the young, "You are lucky to be young . . ."
> Well, not really! To be young today means to have the misfortune of being young.
> This is horrific. This goes against nature. That's evident.
> But that's how things are.
> Why?[1]

[1] *Le Malheur d'être jeune* (Paris: *Les Éditions Nouvelles,* 1935) :8.

Angry and provocative, Valliant-Couturier spent the last seven years of his life writing books dealing with the dilemma of the young during perverse times. Aside from re-publishing *Jean sans Pain* in 1933 with significant changes, he contributed an unusual fable called *Histoire d'Ane pauvre et de Cochon Gras* (The Story of a Poor Donkey and a Fat Pig, 1935) to a new series called *Mon Comrade*, published by Editions Sociales Internationales, which produced modern political books for children. However, 1935 was not a fortunate year for him. An assassination attempt was made on his life. He survived the attack, but two years later, in 1937, he died, apparently due to the repercussions from this attack.

Before his death, as I have mentioned above, Vaillant-Couturier somehow found time in 1933 to rework and re-publish *Jean sans Pain*, deleting some religious motifs and making the book more strident, didactic, and revolutionary. These changes reflect, I believe, Vaillant-Couturier's own transformation, which made him more strident in fighting for socialism, especially after the devastating effects of the Great Depression in 1929 throughout Europe and the rising danger of fascism in Italy, Spain, Germany, and, of course, France throughout the 1930s.

The new edition of *Jean sans Pain*, which serves as the basis for the present English translation, was illustrated by the great innovative artist, Jean Lurçat (1892-1966). His expressionist images are quite different from those of Jean Picart Le Doux (1902-1982), whose watercolor images in the first edition of 1921, are more traditional yet strikingly provocative. This edition is filled with hope that the world can change, while the second edition of 1933 with Lurçat's satirical and somewhat abstract images reveal a godless world in which the bitter struggle to bring about peace and harmony must continue.

Surprisingly, Picart Le Doux, whose final image in the first edition depicted a sunny future with a worker and a peasant shaking hands, was chosen to collaborate with Valliant-Couturier on his satirical picture book, *The Poor Donkey and The Fat Pig.* One would have thought that Valliant-Couturier would have chosen Lurçat because his fable is highly cynical and more in accord with Lurçat's style. However, the collaboration worked because of the gentle way Picart Le Doux depicts the events that lead to the slaughter of the pig. The seemingly serene fable tells a tale about a poor donkey on a farm in the Pyrenees, where Vaillant-Couturier used to spend his summers as a child, and this donkey must cart a supercilious rosy fat pig to the farm after it is bought. The donkey is constantly beaten by the farmer to make him work harder, or he is insulted by the pompous pig who is treated like a king so that he will eat and become fatter for a feast that will take place several months later. The stupid pig is arrogant and mocks the donkey, who becomes somewhat emaciated by all the work he must do, while the pig becomes so fat that it can barely move. At the end of the fable, the donkey is retained and treated better while the pig is slaughtered and roasted for a huge feast. Whether this is really a tale for children is debatable. However, as I have stated, it appeared in a new series of political books for children, and of course, there is a metaphorical lesson to be learned for young and old that pertained to the way laborers were treated in France.

Vaillant-Couturier did not avoid describing the brutality of life for the young. This can be seen in both editions of *Jeans sans Pain*, but neither is as brutal as the fable about the donkey. To a certain extent, the unusual hard learning which Johnny undergoes describes the necessary education that all French youngsters, according to Vaillant-Couturier, needed but never received. The message is heart-felt and sincere.

The reason for the sincerity and emotional appeal of Vaillaint-Couturier's pacifist fairy tale is a strong desire to avoid what he experienced during World War I. In one of his notable essays that he wrote after 1919, he explains:

I learned how to be a solider.

Fifty-two months, I was a soldier for nothing.

However, I grasped what "to serve" meant.

I already had a taste for order. I learned the greatness of discipline and subordination of the individual for the group. The total gift of self-sacrifice.

The tumult of the war, the dreadful waste of international murder, the anarchy of destruction, the savage individualism that ran amuck—all this gave me an intense thirst for a different constructive order. . . .

The order of a new civilization must be larger and embrace the winds of other civilizations.

I was a soldier of entitlement in the company of Sengalese, Madagascans, Anamites, Indians and Hindus. You can imagine the lessons I learned!

Just as I did, they, too, fought for nothing. For worse than nothing, to reinforce the exploitation of their races.

From then on I acquired the passionate desire to be a soldier of a living idea, to obey an agreed upon just discipline, after having first submitted to the mechanical discipline of the bourgeois army.

And so I became a militant. That's to say, a soldier for life. Combatant of the Internationale.[2]

To a great extent, this passage explains the philosophy behind Johnny's coming of age portrayed in Vaillant-Couturier's stunning fairy tale. He was not alone in his effort to develop a new more radical approach to children through literature and painting, and many other European writers joined him in the 1920s, seeking to change the nature of children's literature and speaking truth to power. In one of the most important studies of children's literature between the two world wars, *Écrire pour la jeunesse en France et en Allemagne dans l'entre-deux-guerres (2011),* Mathilde Lévêque cites Vaillant-Couturier's work as the key to understanding the rise of a different children's literature in the twentieth century. Given what one might unfortunately call the misfortune of being young in the twenty-first century, Vaillant-Couturier's fairy tale demands a second life and assessment so that we can all learn how to smile.

---

[2] "Ce que j'ai appris à la guere" in *Vers des lendemains qui chantent* (Paris : Editions Sociales, 1962) : 162.